PRAYER

IN

THE VALLEY

AUTHOR

ROBERT GOINS

PRAYER IN THE VALLEY – Robert Goins

Copyright © 2020

First Edition, First Printing

Printed in the United States of America

ISBN- 979-8-3302-1389-4 (paperback)

ISBN- 979-8-3302-1390-0 (digital)

Author Contact Information:

Robert Goins

http://rgoinsbooks.wix.com

Email:rgoinsbooks@gmail.com

2 SAMUEL 7:28–29

AND NOW, O LORD GOD, THOU
ART THAT GOD AND THY WORDS
BE TRUE, AND THOU HAST
PROMISED THIS GOODNESS UNTO
THY SERVANT: THEREFORE NOW
LET IT PLEASE THEE TO BLESS THE
HOUSE OF THY SERVANT, THAT IT
MAY CONTINUE FOR EVER BEFORE
THEE: FOR THOU, O LORD GOD,
HAST SPOKEN IT: AND WITH THY
BLESSING LET THE HOUSE OF THY
SERVANT BE BLESSED FOREVER.

Contents

INTRODUCTION

As I'm writing this, I am in the midst of things. Like a soldier writing a story to remember that moment; or a letter to his family to stay encouraged in prayer, I feel that I need to write this now.

During this season, I feel the enemy attack even stronger than before. Not just one but many. He is testing every wall of my faith to see where the weak points are. From the knowledge of who I am in Christ, like the temptation he did with Eve. My kids acting out, my marriage, my health, and many more. This place and season don't feel ok. It is far from the peacefulness people describe I should have, even though I know persecution will come and has. I am praying this will help others through hard times when you feel like giving up. But that is not an option! I know you have been praying, but I encourage you to continue and don't grow weary. May this book bless you.

WARNINGS

1 Peter 5:8

Be sober, be vigilant; because your adversary the devil, as a roaring lion, walketh about, seeking whom he may devour.

Sometimes we don't heed the warning signs. When things are going great, it's like the world can't touch us. We don't feel compelled to pray as we use to. We make excuses for the lack of time we have and when we think we are on the right track; we believe nothing can stop us. Then the signs come up, and we see them and say God is in control. We know the enemy attacks, and we allow them to take a little of our peace, time after time, but we think our past prayers have us covered for the new battle. So we quote scripture or sometimes quote words that are just catch phrases, like, "Jesus take the wheel," and the enemy isn't fazed; and we began to wonder, "where is God?"

   We haven't visited God in a while. We do drive-by prayers, and the enemy knows. Soon people around us start going through, loss of loved ones, loss of close relationships, people being incarcerated, or having sicknesses. Now our eyes are on the issues of life, and worry is more prevalent than prayer. We go to pray, and our focus is on everything but Jesus. Little by little, we ignore the attacks, because we see them as insignificant until they pile up, and become so overwhelming. The enemy's purpose is to steal our peace, kill our hope, and destroy our thoughts so we can't focus on God. He knows Jesus is our strength. He knows our peace and sound mind comes from the Prince of Peace. His attacks come like a sprinkle of rain and then a flood, so don't ignore the sprinkles.

Satan doesn't stop trying to steal, kill, or destroy you. Never think the battle is over even though Jesus has the victory, we still have to run the race toward the goal.

Hebrews 12:1-3

Therefore, since we are surrounded by such a great cloud of witnesses, let us throw off everything that hinders and the sin that so easily entangles. And let us run with perseverance the race marked out for us, fixing our eyes on Jesus, the pioneer, and perfecter of faith. For the joy set before him, he endured the cross, scorning its shame, and sat down at the right hand of the throne of God. Consider him who endured such opposition from sinners, so that you will not grow weary and lose heart.

Question

1. What warning signs have you ignored?

2. Has sin crept back in unawares?

3. Do you feel distant from God? Why?

VALLEY

Psalm 23:4

Yea, though I walk through the valley of the shadow of death, I will fear no evil: for thou art with me; thy rod and thy staff they comfort me.

We quote this scripture a lot until we have to walk it. I found that I have no problem with this if it's someone else's valley to walk, but now it's mine. Currently, there are times when I walked the valley with peace, and times when it was overwhelming. The times I've had order, I was already praying. I knew the enemy and his plan from beginning to end because I am walking with Jesus. I was spending time with the One who ordered my steps. He was directing me with His Word. I was so close to Him through prayer; even the still small voice was like a shout. Fear was distant because the love of the Father surrounded me. I know that in the presence of the Lord is the fullness of joy.

I also know that trying to walk the valley without praying and spending time with Jesus is like, running from a killer to get to the light thirty miles away. Your thoughts are on the enemy that tries to catch you and kill you. Every step is a struggle to focus on the light of Jesus. You're tired and keep falling as you hear his shouts and lies. Even the voice of the Lord gets drowned out. I tell you I hate being in this place. But I understand that my lack of prayers at times is why I have lousy valley experiences. Anger, bitterness, unforgiveness, offenses, and fear overtakes us. I forget to be strong and courageous because I lose hope in the promise that, He will never leave me or forsake me (Deuteronomy 31:6). Even though I know greater is He that is in me (1 John 4:4).

If we don't stay in prayer, we shouldn't be surprised when our faith gets lost in our valley moments. Valley moments are unexpected, and you never know when one will show up. Still, your prayer life should already have you prepared for every season. There are times when you are in a valley walk, and you have to pray for others in their valley walk! Are you ready?!

Don't let this season overwhelm you. I found myself complaining about how many people have passed away and the grief I had over friends and family I lost; then I could hear God respond, "How do you think I feel?" It made me sad to think of what God said. How many people left this life not knowing the Father? I was sad for my loss, but what if I had told them about Jesus, and they accepted. Then I will see them again. But if I didn't, and they didn't know Him, then I am not the only one who lost someone, so did God. So many have gotten lost because we get stuck in a circle as we walk in the valley. We get concerned about ourselves instead of Kingdom business, and we lose more than we should. I know it's hard, but use those situations to speak life into others and encourage yourself.

Fear is a liar, and the enemy will vex your spirit to keep you there. Cast off the spirit of fear because it is not from God. How do you do that? By remembering who God is and whose you are. He is Almighty God, and you are His child. He loves you and wants the best for you so much so that He sent Jesus, His only begotten Son, to die for us. That's love, and there is no fear in love. God has you. He always has and He always will.

Questions

1. Are you focused more on your situation or Jesus?

2. Is your tongue speaking life or death?

3. Has the spirit of fear overtaken you as bad things happen to people around you?

CONTINUED PRAYERS

1 Thessalonians 5:17

Pray Without Ceasing.

One thing we can learn from the Israelites is don't get comfortable and ignore God and His will. In peaceful times they began to pray to other gods and give glory to everything else (Jeremiah 2). Not saying we give glory and pray to anything else, but we forget to pray.

Paul tells us to pray without ceasing. He wants us to stay focused on Jesus and not get distracted in our comfort. He knows there is a difference between comfort and rest; That is why Jesus says we will be persecuted for our faith. That we will have tribulation because we are always in a battle. The enemy doesn't want you to finish your race or help others run well; he knows your prayers are important.

Our prayers are essential not only for us but for our family, friends, neighbors, cities, nations, and the world. We must have a continuous prayer life. We can't afford to stop praying. Prayer not only protects us but prepares us for the trial so we can have peace in it. Prayer builds us up for tragedies in life. It gets us ready for the next battle and sustains us in the present struggle. It builds our faith (Jude 1:20-21). Don't stop praying.

I know in this most challenging moment; it is hard to focus. When you prayed all you can pray and asked all the questions, what do you do next?

Romans 8:26-27,

Likewise the Spirit also helps our infirmities: for we know not what we should pray for as we ought: but the

Spirit itself makes intercession for us with groanings which cannot be uttered. And he that searches the hearts knows what is the mind of the Spirit because he makes intercession for the saints according to the will of God.

Pray in the Spirit!! The Spirit knows what to pray through the perfect prayer. Don't dismiss how the Word is teaching you how to pray. If we pray in the Spirit, we know that everything is working out for our good.

Romans 8:28,

And we know that all things work together for good to them that love God, to them who are the called according to his purpose.

Your Spirit man knows that you have a purpose, and you need to pray in the Spirit to overcome those fears and worries. God is moving on your behalf as you pray with the groanings of the Spirit. Let your prayers be fervent and with faith.

Questions

1. How is your prayer life?

2. What excuses have kept you from

   praying?

3. How important is prayer to you?

IN THE TRENCHES
Ephesians 6:11

Put on the whole armor of God, that ye may be able to stand against the wiles of the devil.

How does it feel in the trenches? Horrible!! I can't sugarcoat it, being sick, losing loved ones, loss of finances, struggles with relationships, and so on, is not fun! It is not the way we pictured this Christian walk. We wondered if there was a fine print area we missed. No, it was the red print we ignored.

John 16:33

These things I have spoken unto you, that in me ye might have peace. In the world ye shall have tribulation: but be of good cheer; I have overcome the world.

The world will hate us because of Jesus, remember that. How about the scripture in Revelation when the serpent made war against the children of God (Revelation 12:17)? Sometimes we forget, and it feels good to be able to enjoy the rest periods. We hope the enemy will leave us alone, but we know he will not. You have to be ready to move forward, or you will fall back.

Our goal is to move forward and take more land, but if fear takes over because of lack of prayer, we will turn back to old trenches or stay where we are and starve from lack of nourishment. Remember, fear is not from God (2 Timothy 1:7). We must be courageous and not forget the people who are in the trenches with us. We must remember the trenches are a temporary place, and it serves a purpose to prepare us to take more ground. We cannot linger in it for long. Strategies through prayer are received to gain more ground from the enemy, if not for you, but others in the body of Christ. It is not a (me) battle, but a Kingdom battle. We are following the commandments from the King of Kings.

God's perfect love cast out fear (1 John 4:18). When we remember His love for us, we remember His truth in us. Meditate on the truth of God and cast down the lies of the enemy. God loves you and walks with you in the valley. He prepares a table for you before your enemies because they don't have the power to take it as long as you trust Him and don't fear. Stand firm in the faith with the truth of who Jesus is. He is all-powerful and merciful. Trust Him!!

The process of the trenches is getting you to trust God and get out of the way. It is where you move from a carnal mind to a spiritual mind. It is where iron sharpens iron, through other believers. This process is separating and disconnecting fear and putting on trust and faith in Jesus. How much of His Word do you believe? In the trenches, your weapon is not just the Word, but now you have to use it in faith. Taking God at His Word!! He said it, it's true, "I am healed! I will prosper! I will live and not die! I will see the goodness of God in the land of the living!!" The blood of Christ saved us; do you believe that? Jesus gave us life more abundant; do you believe that?

Satan tried to use the Word on Jesus, but Jesus knew His sword and used it to defeat the temptations of the enemy. We have to do the same. Every Word of God is true, and if we get to know the Word of God, then we know God and the strength He has to prepare us in the trenches in the valley.

Questions

1. What is the full armor of God?

2. Do you wear your armor daily?

3. Are you willing to go through the process?

NOT ALONE

Hebrews 13:5

Let your conversation be without covetousness; and be content with such things as ye have: for he hath said, I will never leave thee, nor forsake thee.

As I mentioned, we are not alone in the trenches. Don't be afraid to reach out to others for prayer. We struggle and need other warriors to fight with us. Don't let shame, pride, guilt, offenses, or any other lie the enemy says, stop you from reaching out to others. You are not alone! Jesus said where two or three are gathered in His name; He is present. He knows there is power in numbers. We need each other, not only in hard times but in joyous times. We need to spend time praying with and for each other. We need to fellowship with each other to build our relationships, so when hard times come, we can, with confidence, call on each other for help. We lift each other up daily in prayer and words that encourage. We put on the full armor of God and also watch each other's back. We are stronger together, especially when fear and doubt arise; we can speak into one another and dispel the lies, by speaking the truth in love. This walk to glory isn't a lone one even if it feels like we are in it by ourselves; there are many more who are needing us.

We are reminded not to forsake the assembling of ourselves (Hebrews 10:25). We have to know each other beyond the church walls. We live secret lives, and Satan uses it to conquer us one by one. We are stronger together! We desire to see each other prosper, so we pray for one another. Don't let going to church be the only time you fellowship with brothers and sisters of Christ. Build lasting and loving relationships. Not afraid of offending or being offended, seeing that God has graced us with repentance and forgiveness. We will all make a mistake and hurt each other, at times, but we as Christians should know how to repent and forgive each other (John 20:22-23).

We are one body in Christ. Paul makes it clear in

1 Corinthians 12 how we are many members, but one body. No one is separate.

1 Corinthians 12:12-13,

For as the body is one, and hath many members, and all the members of that one body, being many, are one body: so also is Christ. For by one Spirit are we all baptized into one body, whether we be Jews or Gentiles, whether we be bond or free; and have been all made to drink into one Spirit.

He also let us know that even the parts of the body we think are less honorable, God has given abundant honor (See vs. 23-24).

Don't let pride keep you alone in the fight. We mourn and rejoice together; let us also fight together. Let's keep each other lifted in prayer daily, showing love to one another. Remember, iron sharpens iron, so let us sharpen each other's weapons for the battles in our lives.

Questions

1. Is pride keeping you from reaching out to others?

2. Do you feel you're the only One going through?

3. Are you holding onto unforgiveness?

FEW ARE CHOSEN
Matthew 22:14

For many are called, but few are chosen.

I have learned over the years that I have many people I can call, but there are only a few I choose when it comes to prayer. Jesus calls a lot of people, but only a few will respond, and the rest will miss their call. When you need prayer, you need someone who will pray, NOW!

I have a lot of friends, but I have some that will pray earnestly right now and others who will say I will pray for you. I do not discard their prayers, because I know that they will pray in a passing thought or when they have time to do so. Even though you are not alone, understand who has a desire for you to overcome and who doesn't. You need those prayer warriors who speak life and want to see you in victory. Stay away from people who will speak the worse scenario into your life. Those who give you a prison sentence, death sentence, or even laugh at you. Be careful who you tell about your situation. Even Jesus had to put people out who laughed Him to scorn (Matthew 9:25). You have to put them out of your circle of people you tell about your valley experiences. They have to mature. Jesus had twelve disciples, but only allowed three with Him at times, Peter, James, and John, the brother of James. On the Mount of transfiguration (Matthew 17:1), when Jesus raised the little girl from the dead (Mark 5:35), and in the garden of Gethsemane (Matthew 26:36). Even though they spoke out of turn, fell asleep, also ran away, Jesus trusted them to be there in those times when doubt and fear could overtake Him. Know who you can take into the valley that will help pray you through it.

The effectual fervent prayer of a righteous man availeth much (James 5:16). Look to righteous effectually zealous prayer warriors! Who are they? Those who have become the righteousness of God through faith in Jesus Christ (Romans 3:22). They know they are His, and believe what they ask, will be received. If someone starts off giving you doctors to contact or tell you about a person they lost, you may need to pray for them. Yes, people have lost a lot of money, loved ones, and relationships, but this doesn't have to be you. You need someone who will interrupt you during your story and begin to pray. The only detail they need is that your situation is disrupting your peace. Let Christ be the first suggestion and let the Holy Spirit give you the direction to go. If it is a doctor, excellent, God has given them wisdom in medicine. If it is a bank or other financial institution, do it, let investors who have the knowledge you don't have invest for you. If you need a counselor, go, and get them to give you sound advice; just remember God first.

The more you broadcast your issues to the wrong people, the more word curses may get spoken over your situation. People share a lot of their problems on social media, and strangers are speaking over their situation for good and evil. King Hezekiah showed his whole kingdom to Babylon, and all his stuff and he lost it all (2 Kings 20:12-19). Not in his lifetime, but in his sons. Be careful what you share and with whom you share it with, because not every close friend has your best interest at hand (Psalm 41:9).

I am not writing this as an unfriend, everyone, you can't trust chapter. I am saying, don't call an electrician to do your plumbing. You have people in your life who fulfills what you need in certain areas at specific times. Peter, James, and John were with Jesus alone in situations, but Jesus never said to the other nine," I don't need you." Everyone had a purpose, even Judas. Judas' betrayal was the purpose of the way to salvation. Because the deception was necessary so

Jesus would receive chastisement for your peace, they mocked and rejected Him that you may be accepted. Bruised and wounded for your healing transgressions and iniquities. Judged through unrighteousness that you may have righteousness in Christ. Nailed to a cross to remove the curse of sin by His blood. Died to defeat death that you may live. He arose from the dead with all power and authority that you may rise in Spirit. Ascended to the Father and intercedes on your behalf. Also given to us, who are adopted into the family of the King, the Holy Spirit to guide, comfort, and correct us. Everyone allowed in your life has a purpose. Ask God what it is and for how long. Your walk in Christ maybe what they need, or their walk may be what you need. Iron sharpens iron!

Question

1. Who do you know will pray fervently for you? Make a list.

2. Can others count on you to pray fervently for them?

3. Is Jesus your first choice to go to when issues happen?

4. How much info do you share on social media?

VICTORY IN PRAYER
1 Corinthians 15:57

But thanks be to God! He gives us the victory through our Lord Jesus Christ.

How do you win this battle? Pray, pray, and pray. It is the one thing you must continue until you have victory. Jesus said, "If I am lifted up, I will draw all men unto me (John 12:32)." Jesus wants us to lift Him up with prayer in our heart, so our focus is stayed on Him. Prayer brings us into His rest. The disciples asked Jesus to teach them one important thing, that is how to pray (Luke 11:1-4). They knew His prayer life was what brought the manifestation of deliverance, peace, healing, and love. Even before the cross, He spent the night in prayer to overcome His will to surrender to the Father's will. It was a tough challenge for Jesus to take the cross, but He overcame through prayer. Before the arrest, the betrayal, the slap, and spit in His face; before the false accusations, the whips, and thorns; before the judgment, the cross, and feeling forsaken, He prepared himself to forgive in prayer. We have to prepare ourselves with prayers for every attack and have forgiveness readily on our hearts and lips.

We cannot overcome without prayer. We cannot continue with prayers only at bedtime, morning, wake up, or when we eat. We need fervent prayers that are continuous and intentional. The enemy is deliberate with his attacks, so we have to be deliberate with our prayers, keeping on our hearts and minds the promises and visions of God. If He said it, then it is so. We can be like Eve and give our ear to the lie, or we can stand in the trust of God. I will trust Jesus no matter what it looks and feels at this moment. I believe that God's standard is mightier than the flood of the enemy. He is our strong tower, our strength, our hope, and He is making everything work out for our good. Trust in Him. Trust in the Lord.

Prayer is our lifeline to Jesus. It is what keeps us up on what He is saying at this moment. Have you ever had a friend you never talk too? What have you not received from them from a lack of communication? What have you missed? When you speak to them, you may say how you need to catch up? Don't make

Jesus that type of friend. Stay in touch with Him all through the day (Psalm 16:8).

Prayer is how we seek wisdom and understanding. It is how we get strategies on how to overcome the battle. David would seek God on whether to fight battles and get instructions on how to go about doing it (2 Samuel 5:19). Even when David's family got captured, and the men wanted to kill him, he inquired of the Lord whether he should pursue or not (1 Samuel 30). What would you do if someone takes your family and others want to kill you? Will you panic and give chase or seek an answer from God? If you are like me, give chase and not seek what God says. I am learning to trust God more without giving into fear. I am in process as I go from faith to faith (Romans 1:17), from strength to strength, from glory to glory (2 Corinthians 3:16-18). As the father of the child said, Lord, I believe, Lord help my unbelief (Mark 9:24). We believe but have disbelief in some areas, and God wants to bring us to the fullness of faith and trust in His Word. Without faith, we cannot please Him.

Questions

1. Do you have a little faith or no faith?

2. How do you feel when you pray compared to when you don't pray?

3. What battles have you overcome through prayer?

TESTIMONY
Revelation 12:11

And they overcame him by the blood of the Lamb and by the Word of their testimony, and they loved not their lives unto the death.

As I said before, this type of season is rough. But if I didn't surround myself with people of faith, I would have given up. I would be stuck in, all things are possible, except for my situation. That is a lie the enemy wants you to have. God will never leave you, and all things are possible, even my case. We forget who we are in Christ, and without others, it is easy for us to fear and worry. It's not good to get bad news. A doctor's diagnosis, a phone call of a passing relative or friend, break up or divorce; being rejected, loss of finances or home. When your peace gets disrupted, it is hard to stay calm. But remember that you are walking with Jesus. Testify as how good He is, even in the valley, there is a table He has prepared. See how wonderful He is? Even among your enemies, His focus is on taking care of you. He isn't worried about your enemy taking anything from your table. I can testify now about our holy and mighty God. I can put my mind on His promises and purposes for my life. I tasted of goodness at the table of healing, deliverance, provision, and love, and know that the LORD is good. Soon the situation starts to break, and I can see the hills.

I begin to climb the hills, and I feel gladness and hope, then I get pulled back in the valley with another situation. Now it feels like a rollercoaster ride, but I remembered what I came through. I began to testify to myself of what God has already done. I start quoting His promises. Even though I'm on this rollercoaster ride, I'm encouraged and empowered with trust in the Lord. My change in the situation does not change my God.

Every step is a testimony. As David sacrificed after those six steps (2 Samuel 6:13), my testimony is a sacrifice to give God praise for the little even before I see the fullness of it. We overcome by the blood of the Lamb and the Word of our testimony (Revelation 12:11). We also have not to love our lives unto death.

What does that mean? That means to get our minds off our situations and focus on God. When we're thinking about our circumstances, we worry and ask, when God, why God, or how God? Instead of your will, God, either way, I trust you.

If I trust God, that means I trust His decision, plan, and timing. I know we want it to be over with, but to rush God is to find fault with Him. Paul understood that he was bonded with Christ, whether in this life or the next (Philippians 1:21-23). He knew the goal is to be with Christ for eternity. Our eternity starts the moment we accept Christ as our Lord and Savior. That means right now; I have the blood of the Lamb; I have a testimony, and I have conquered my fear of death through Jesus Christ.

Now I know that the anointing comes after the table. I have to ignore the devil and focus on Jesus, even when the shifting starts. I have to react to my enemies with love, joy, peace, patience, kindness, goodness, faithfulness, gentleness, and self-control. I do this because I received it through Jesus. He is anointing my head with oil as I give him my full attention. It doesn't matter whether good or bad, keep your eyes on Jesus.

Questions

1. What testimonies do you remember from God's faithfulness?

2. Are you getting weary? Why?

3. What scriptures help you to be encouraged? Focus on them.

JESUS IS FOR YOU

Romans 8:31

What shall we then say to these things? If God is for us, who can be against us?

One thing you must always remember is, Jesus is fighting for you. You must focus on God and not on the situation. Amid frustration and bad news, we get sidetracked from God and start focusing on the worst scenarios. The bible tells us to focus on things that are true, honest, just, pure, lovely, of good report, with any virtue, and having any praise, to think on these things (Philippians 4:8).

Because we become transformed into what our minds think on mostly. I was praying in the Spirit when I heard the Lord give me the Scripture Romans 3:4. Of course, I had to look it up. The first thing I notice is to let God be true and every man a liar. I knew that His Word was right, but I wasn't letting it reign true in my life; I know He cannot lie, but I was holding on to the lie of the enemy.

The Word says I am healed because of His stripes, but I wasn't receiving it. It's also written that He has taken on our infirmities and sickness, but my faith wasn't there. As I started to do as the Bible instructs us to do, meditate on the Word, and focus on the truth, my situation began to change. I have to keep His Word in front of me to remember.

Isaiah 53:4-5,

Surely, he hath borne our griefs and carried our sorrows: yet we did esteem him stricken, smitten of God, and afflicted. But he was wounded for our transgressions; he was bruised for our iniquities: the chastisement of our peace was upon him, and with his stripes, we are healed.

Everything that God says in His Word is true, so whose report will you believe?! You will prosper as your soul prosper (3 John 1:2). We are blessed, and Jesus has come to give us life more abundantly (John 10:10). As we behold God, meditating on His Word and praying daily, we are transformed into His image (2 Corinthians 3:18). I forgot this precept myself, and God reminded me of who I was to Him. He instructed me to pray and seek Him. So I did. I found my peace again. Even in the valley, I found that the Prince of Peace truly never leaves me or forsakes me. I had to cast off the spirit of fear and vexation that took away my focus and give my attention back to the One who gives peace, joy, love, kindness, wisdom, and so much more!!

I know the process is rough, but it is necessary to mold you into who God wants you to be. The valley is a route you have to travel to get to where God has planned, but remember that Jesus sent the Holy Spirit to guide and comfort you. You're not alone; keep your eyes on the Almighty!!

Questions

1. Do you trust God's Word?

2. Who is God trying to be to you in this situation?

3. Do you spend time meditating on His Word? How much?

AUTHOR'S LAST WORDS

I hope this book helps you as you walk through your valley. It is a complicated process, but it brings forth the plan God has for you. God knows the enemy will attack, and He has already put a plan of escape and strategies for victory beforehand. If we keep our eyes and thoughts on Jesus, we will be stronger than when we started.

The big question is, do you trust who God is. I can hear His voice ring in my ears, "Do you trust me?" My response is yes, Lord, but my actions sometimes are, no Lord. I find the battle between my Spirit man and my flesh man becomes real in the valley; now I have to pray that my Spirit man wins the battle. To win, I have to get help from the Holy Spirit and the Body of Christ! The Holy Spirit directs and corrects me through the process, and the prayers of the Saints are the strongest because the Lord finds joy when we pray for each other, and His joy strengthens me.

I've considered today and how it's filled with His Spirit. Yet, if I focus on my issues, I receive what my problems can give me, fear, anxiety, frustration, and more. I chose the Spirit of God. I decided to commune with the Father and focus on Him and His promises.

When trouble arises like a need for money or a ride when your car breaks down, do you go to someone who hates you or to a reliable friend? So when trouble arises, why do we go to fear and stress? Why do we go to frantic and panic? Go to Jesus, who gives peace. This valley is where I learned to go to the One who has peace during the storm. The One who comforts and provides wisdom that I may have life abundantly. Is it easy? No, but it is possible. Keep praying and meditating on the Word of God and know, no matter what, you already have provision, protection, healing, and peace. You have victory in the valley because God hears your prayers, even in the valley!!

YOU ARE BLESSED AND A BLESSING!! REMEMBER WHOSE YOU ARE AND WHO YOU ARE!!

www.ingramcontent.com/pod-product-compliance
Lightning Source LLC
Chambersburg PA
CBHW072114150726
47999CB00005B/2016